A GIFT FROM MY FATHER

A Tribute to the Greatest Generation

MICHAEL L. BANNER

A Gift from My Father

Cover design by Rtor Maghuyop

Interior design by Jomel Pepito

Published in the United States of America

1 Family & Relationships/Panning/Fatherhood

2. Family & Relationships Ethics de Mon

12.10.04

Dedication

Many people don't realize that the greatest generation has been "the greatest generation" for a very long time. In recent years, the term seems to be used more often than it has been in the past. Certainly, Tom Brokaw's incredible book, The Greatest Generation, published in 2001, should be given much credit for keeping the recognition and respect of this extraordinary group of Americans in American society, but that was over 20 years ago… And it's time for another reminder.

There are other factors that have contributed to this trend as well. Movies like Pearl Harbor and, my personal favorite, Saving Private Ryan, were not only tributes to that generation, but their vivid reenactment of that period of time allowed children, grandchildren, nieces, and nephews to see just how courageous their parents, grandparents, aunts, and uncles really acted. Their pride in their country was the foundation for building America.

I was blessed to have a father from this generation. He asked his parents for permission to enlist in the Army or Air Force at the age of seventeen. He was a tail gunner in a B-24 and was shot down over Austria. He was held in a German prison camp for fourteen months. Being Jewish, surviving this was no small feat. He came home in 1945 as a decorated war hero, became an entrepreneur before that word gained its current popularity, lived a just-do-it life decades before Nike was ever heard of, and was an incredible example of what that generation stood for. He lived by a set of rules and guidelines that his generation stood for.

It amazes me how that generation's guidelines still apply today. In fact, they may be more important than ever, considering the incredibly difficult times so many are now facing in this great country. However, it amazes me even more how many people today consider those guidelines outdated, old-fashioned, and too corny to apply in today's incredibly modern, fast-paced world.

This book is going to list those guidelines. It will even make some pithy comments about each one. It will also have pictures representing a lifetime of being an incredible father, grandfather, husband, and man.

It is the perspective of the son of a father from the greatest generation.

Acknowledgment

So many people to thank…

My three children:

My son **Joshua**, who has grown into such an incredible, caring, intelligent and thoughtful young man. (And he has watched Star Trek with me since he was born!)

My daughter **Tabatha**, the best Mom in the world, shows me every day that love is stronger than blood.

My daughter **Staci**, who is the most like my father and is the closest thing to a real Supergirl this planet has to offer.

My cousin **Bob Banner**, who is more like my brother and is possibly the only other person in the world who had a relationship with his father like I had with mine.

Ira Bronsky, my own personal savior, more family than friends, a brother, a confidant. Where would I be without this man…

Peter Gelbwaks, more family than friends, a confidant, a teacher, a mentor, the best example of being a father and grandfather. (When you are Peter's friend, opportunities are limitless).

Craig Corn, a great friend, teacher, confidant, who allowed me to appear to so many people that I was much smarter than I actually was. (I guess the secret is out now)

Torrey Larsen, a great friend with that rare quality of making anyone he touches a better person. He certainly did that for me…

Liane Bennati, to say more family than a friend would be the understatement of the year. The perfect example of a friend, a mom and a daughter. She also had a father of the Greatest Generation who was her hero, and I loved him so much.

Nadine & Ali Ismail, two of the most caring people I have ever met, who have also gone from acquaintances to friends to family. Knowing them, and their three wonderful children, has been a blessing to myself and my family.

Table of Contents

Dedication ... iii

Acknowledgment ... v

Foreword ... x

The Greatest Generation Looks Directly in Your Eyes When It Speaks to You ... 1

The Greatest Generation Has a Firm Handshake ... 2

The Greatest Generation Says What It Means and Means What It Says ... 3

The Greatest Generation Supports Its Family ... 4

The Greatest Generation Doesn't Tell Its Children at a Certain Age that They Are No Longer Their Responsibility ... 5

The Greatest Generation Puts Up Or Shuts Up ... 7

The Greatest Generation Is Not Afraid of Risk! ... 8

The Greatest Generation Has Manners ... 9

The Greatest Generation Never Gives Up ... 10

The Greatest Generation Always Competes to Win ... 11

The Greatest Generation Doesn't Believe, "It's the Thought That Counts." ... 12

The Greatest Generation Never Kicks a Man When He Is Down ... 13

The Greatest Generation Gives to Those Less Fortunate, and Many Times It Does It Anonymously 14

The Greatest Generation Is Full of Patriots! 15

The Greatest Generation Votes 16

The Greatest Generation Teaches Its Children to Respect a Police Uniform and the Men and Women Who Wear It 17

The Greatest Generation Doesn't Do Drugs Or Get Drunk in Front of Its Children 18

The Greatest Generation Isn't Late! 19

The Greatest Generation Doesn't Whine 20

The Greatest Generation Has Opinions 21

The Greatest Generation Doesn't Go Dutch! 22

The Greatest Generation Learns from Its Mistakes 23

The Greatest Generation Pays Child Support 26

The Greatest Generation Strives for More 27

The Greatest Generation Is as Good as Its Word 28

The Greatest Generation Leads by Example 29

The Greatest Generation Doesn't Wear Makeup Or Other Girly Products 30

The Greatest Generation Makes People Feel Good 31

The Men of the Greatest Generation Are Still Little Boys at Heart....32

The Greatest Generation Has So Many Real Friends....33

The Greatest Generation Has Goals Most Feel Are Unreachable Or Unrealistic....34

The Greatest Generation Believes Imagination Is Stronger Than Knowledge....35

The Greatest Generation Believes in Hard Work....36

The Greatest Generation Knows Real Power Is Never Given, Real Power Is Taken....37

And, Finally, the Greatest Generation Knows the Power of Having the Right Woman....38

About The Author....53

Foreword

Dad never became a millionaire, but we wanted for nothing and certainly had more than most. We were inseparable from when I was very young until he left us on May 5, 2005, in his bedroom in my home, surrounded by those who loved him.

A couple of days after his death, as I sat and wrote his eulogy, I realized what started out as a eulogy turned into a tribute to my father and his entire generation. He had rules, he had guidelines, and they never changed. He lived by these rules, and he imparted them to his son every chance he had. And now, I impart them to my children and grandchildren, and I am damn proud to do so.

He was my best friend, mentor, coach, teacher, and personal banker; he was a rock when all things around him were unsteady. He was my hero, my Superman. He believed in truth, justice, and the American way. He was one of the best the greatest generation had to offer.

The Greatest Generation Looks Directly in Your Eyes When It Speaks to You

This was one of Dad's favorites. Believe this one! Live it. Be it. The person who doesn't look you in the eyes when he speaks to you is lying. Run away from this person.

In my career and personal life, I have hired hundreds of people. Every time I have ignored this advice, I have regretted it.

The Greatest Generation Has a Firm Handshake

If you gave my dad a weak, limp handshake, it would take a miracle to overcome that terrible first impression...

They say a weak handshake equals a weak conviction; they are right!

(By the way, while shaking your hand firmly, they'd better look directly into your eyes!)

The Greatest Generation Says What It Means and Means What It Says

It's often said but rarely lived. My Dad didn't mince words. It offended some people, but you always knew where you stood.

I like this style instead of today's politically correct "I'm afraid I might offend someone if I actually tell you what I am thinking." Nonsense.

The Greatest Generation Supports Its Family

There's no such thing as:

"I can't find a job in my field,"

"My boss doesn't like me,"

"I'm burned out."

These types of men drove my dad crazy his entire life. Although Dad was self-employed his entire life, how many times did he take an extra job when bad times hit? Was he embarrassed? No, he was proud to support and provide for his family!

There is no better proof of this great quality than today when you walk into a major store and are greeted by a senior at the entrance asking you if you need a cart or a fast-food chain where you will see a senior at the counter, right next to the teenager, asking you if you would like fries with your meal. These incredible seniors found themselves short on income, so what did they do? They came out of retirement and got a job! What an incredible attitude this generation still has today.

The Greatest Generation Doesn't Tell Its Children at a Certain Age that They Are No Longer Their Responsibility

They know being a father is a lifetime commitment. Just what happened to this philosophy? Today's politically correct and, in many cases, just plain lazy parents are so worried about enabling their children that they are stopping short of their responsibilities.

When one of my children finds themselves in a bad situation, regardless of the circumstances and regardless of their age, they know I am there. And they will know that until I leave this earth.

Thanks, Dad (and Mom), for passing that parenting skill on to me. There are simply too many examples of this throughout my life that my father proved true for me to choose just one. One example that does stand out actually involved his grandson, my son Joshua.

Joshua's twelfth birthday party was just days before Dad left us. We were going to cancel, but Dad insisted we not. The day before the party, Dad called me in his room and handed me a cheque for one hundred dollars. He said, "Go cash this and get a brand new one-hundred-dollar bill. I want to give it to Josh before he leaves for his party."

In a hospital bed in his room, with twenty-four-hour hospice care and the morphine drip flowing, he still wanted to bring a smile to his grandson's face. That was my children's "Poppy".

The Greatest Generation Puts Up Or Shuts Up

In other words, money talks and s—t walks! It's crude, blunt, and offends most people, but it's true.

If you believe in yourself or you believe in a certain idea of yours, and you won't risk your own money, then you don't really believe, do you?

The Greatest Generation Is Not Afraid of Risk!

The cliché "No guts, no glory" describes them so well.

They knew that in order to achieve incredible goals, they had to take incredible risks. This certainly was proven when they enlisted in mass for World War II.

But it doesn't stop there.

They returned home victorious to a nation that was going through a very serious post-war depression just a few years after the Great Depression.

They opened businesses at a startling rate, bought homes at a startling rate, and returned to college at a startling rate.

They cured diseases, they broke racial barriers, and they created the backbone of the greatest country the world had ever known.

The Greatest Generation Has Manners

When did opening a car door for a woman, picking up the check, giving up your seat on a bus or train, and not using vile language go out of style?

The Greatest Generation never stopped! By the way, all of you incredibly modern women, this is not chauvinism. It's chivalry!

The Greatest Generation Never Gives Up

Rocky Balboa said it best: “It’s not about how many times you get hit; it’s about how many times you can get hit and keep moving forward.”

The Greatest Generation never failed; they just didn’t always succeed on schedule.

This is one of the attributes that made them the greatest generation!

Dad just didn’t give up; it wasn’t in him to do so. Again, there are a lifetime of examples to choose from, but I have to skip to the very end of his life. Among other problems, Dad developed congestive heart failure in the last 18 months of his life. He had 5 heart attacks and several infections, including one going septic. In each case, the ER Doctor would inform us that the odds were greatly against my father surviving and “it was time to call the family in.”

And in each case, Dad went home, insisted on returning to physical therapy, and made a comeback! He just wasn’t ready to leave us...

The Greatest Generation Always Competes to Win

This is one of those touchy-feely, politically correct things that made my father, and still makes me want to throw up! Yes, we should always play by the rules. Yes, you always shake the hand of the man who beat you. But if you are not there to win, you shouldn't be there in the first place.

When I hear parents say, "Oh, winning doesn't mean anything. I just want them to have a good time," or "I don't want to put too much pressure on them," I feel so sorry for those kids. The real world will eat them up.

My God, the greatest generation believed and lived this.

Whether it's sports, business, or a game of Monopoly, I compete to win. It annoys many. They too often confuse it with "the need to win." They are so missing the point. It's about trying your best all the time, every time. When you do this, not only do you win much more than most, but, more importantly, when you lose, you lose with pride, with no embarrassment. You shake the hand of the person who beat you, and you can't wait for the next challenge.

I consider this philosophy a lifetime gift from my Dad.

The Greatest Generation Doesn't Believe, "It's the Thought That Counts."

It's not the thought that counts. It never has been. It's the action that counts!

If you are thinking of doing something good, whether for yourself or others, and you're capable of doing it, and you don't do it, what the heck good was the thought? Thoughts don't change the world.

Thoughts don't bring leaders to the forefront of our society.

Thoughts don't cure diseases. Thoughts are only the beginning of greatness.

Action is what counts!

The Greatest Generation Never Kicks a Man When He Is Down

My dad and I spent so much time together when I was growing up that I often saw him approached by someone down on their luck. After listening to this person's tale of woe, I always fully expected my father to reply with his normal, positive, and often very strong "Stop feeling sorry for yourself and fix the problem" attitude. (After all, that's what I would have heard.) I was always amazed how Dad would either reach into his pocket to help solve this man's problems or go out of his way to help him in another way.

When I questioned Dad on this, his reaction was always the same: "You never kick a man when he is down."

The Greatest Generation Gives to Those Less Fortunate, and Many Times It Does It Anonymously

It doesn't have to be money. It can be time. Be a coach, be a big brother, and do what you can, but do!

Today, many of the younger generations consider it "good karma."

The greatest generation did it simply because it was right.

My Dad gave for the sake of giving, as did so many of his generation. It always amazes me that so many "givers" today want the "recognition" that usually comes with that giving. I applaud their spirit, but I think the art of giving "for the sake of giving" seems to have become extinct.

The Greatest Generation Is Full of Patriots!

This is an important one. You can be a Republican, and you can be a Democrat. You can be a liberal or a conservative; you can be on the left or the right, but if you don't believe that the United States of America is the greatest country on the planet, then shut up! Or better yet, get out.

Today's very volatile circumstances throughout the world make this one so important. As this book is being created, this great country is more divided than those who serve it!

You have every right to support the reasons for us being involved on foreign soil or not! That's what makes this country so great.

But whether you support this country's position or not, you'd better support the incredible men and women serving their country!

The Greatest Generation Votes

If you are not going to participate in the number-one activity that separates this country from the rest, you should just keep your mouth shut.

Enough said….

The Greatest Generation Teaches Its Children to Respect a Police Uniform and the Men and Women Who Wear It

Another lost art, and I blame the parents. My father taught me very early that law enforcement people were there to help you, and the only people who did not like or respect them were probably doing something against the law.

The attitude of so many people in this country towards our law enforcement men and women literally sickens me, and it would sicken my father as well.

The Greatest Generation Doesn't Do Drugs Or Get Drunk in Front of Its Children

It just amazes me how many people get drunk or even do drugs with their children. Or just how many parents today use alcohol or drugs to cope with their lives. They may not all be perfect, but the great, great majority of them are always there to "Protect and Serve."

Just what has happened to today's society? I saw my father drink on many occasions throughout our life. But I can honestly say I never saw him "drunk." I never saw him behave in any way that would embarrass me or him. There were never any stories that started with "I was so drunk that I...." Today's parents seem to be so proud of their "wilder days." I just don't get it.

The Greatest Generation Isn't Late!

If you don't have respect for your own time, at least have some respect for the other person's time!

Being on time was one of my father's pet peeves. It was not one of my mother's. This was a constant source of aggravation to him but also a constant source of amusement to me.

Dad hated being late for anything! Mom thought that time was some sort of an estimate of when something might just start, a suggestion at best! For fifty-plus years, they argued over that, and for fifty-plus years, it was as if they had never argued about it before. But they were married fifty-plus years. What a generation!

The Greatest Generation Doesn't Whine

If something goes wrong, take it on the chin and just keep going.

Tony Robbins says it best: "The man who is always saying, 'I should have done that, I should have done this,' looks back on his life and realizes he 'should all over himself." The greatest generation never whined.

Dad hated whiners. If one of his friends or I started the whining process, just the look on Dad's face would remind us that this conversation was falling on deaf ears.

For those of you bleeding hearts out there, it didn't mean he didn't care about the problems being whined about. He just wanted us to get past the whining part and get to the solving-the-problem part.

The Greatest Generation Has Opinions

And they are not afraid to stick by them.

"I'm on the fence on that one,"

"I agree with both sides,"

"I really do see both points of view,"

"That's a rough one."

Give me a break. Choose a side and take a position!

This was not only one of Dad's pet peeves, but he definitely passed this one on to me. This one just kills me! Whether we are discussing politics or just looking at a menu, when an adult "just can't decide," it drives me crazy.

The Greatest Generation Doesn't Go Dutch!

Never! If you can't afford to take a woman out on a date, don't ask her! This is not chauvinism, and it is chivalry. (Another lost art).

Dutch? Are you kidding me? I am hoping many women read this book. If a man wants to go Dutch on a date, cancel the date! And again, this is not chauvinism; it's chivalry! (Look it up!)

The Greatest Generation Learns from Its Mistakes

This was one of their greatest attributes. The greatest generation was known for their self-confidence, yet when they made a mistake, they corrected it, moved on, and kept their pride intact, a talent some of the younger generations seem to have forgotten.

The greatest generation knew that failing at something was not a bad thing. Giving up was unacceptable. Today's "instant gratification" generation seems to have forgotten that past failures magically turn into stepping stones to success when you ultimately achieve your goal. Just don't give up!

The Greatest Generation Says Yes, You Can Sometimes Judge A Book By Its Cover

I know, you're saying people shouldn't do that.

Most don't realize the original cliché the greatest generation created was actually, "You shouldn't **always** judge a book by its cover." This I agree with.

But somehow, certain tattooed, pierced, multi-colored haired, mohawked, gold-toothed, pants-falling-down-below-their-butt, "I know I look and act like I'm from a different planet, but how dare you treat me like it" group of people decided to take the word "always" out of this age-old and more- often-true-than-not cliché! Well, how convenient.

You are judged in this world by many things, and your appearance is one of them. Just one more thing on this one.

When you walk into a library and thousands, tens of thousands, and in some cases, hundreds of thousands of books, they all have covers!

(And the cookbooks don't have a skull and crossbones on the cover) Think about it.

Just must add another comment to this one. In recent years, I have learned that “always judging a book by its cover” can be a terrible mistake. (Thanks Staci!)

The Greatest Generation Pays Child Support

Although the divorce rate of the greatest generation was at a staggering low compared to today's statistics:

They didn't "hide their real income."

They didn't "pay as little as possible."

They didn't say, "My kids have everything they need at my house."

They wanted their children to have the highest quality of life, whatever home they lived in.

The greatest generation knew you divorced your wife, never your children!

The Greatest Generation Strives for More

Their goals were unusually high, and if they met those goals earlier than expected, they didn't rest on their laurels.

They raised the bar.

Dad never stopped encouraging me: not "pushing" but encouraging. There is a big difference. If you strive for mediocrity, that's where you usually end up.

The Greatest Generation Is as Good as Its Word

Like other great words, these are often said but not lived by enough. Their words were their bond. Another lost art.

The greatest generation lived by this. That's why they were trusted; that's why today they are revered by so many still today. If Dad gave me his word, he would keep it. A constant in a world filled with variables can make a child, a friend, or a business partner know that they can always depend on you.

The Greatest Generation Leads by Example

Every now and then, especially when you are a parent, you find yourself saying, “Do as I say, not as I do.”

But in the end, it will always come back to haunt you.

The greatest generation definitely led by example.

The Greatest Generation Doesn't Wear Makeup Or Other Girly Products

Obviously, I'm referring to the men. This one just killed my Dad. I refuse to even say another word.

But…. when my Dad or one of his friends had a formal affair to attend, they all made appointments for manicures. Hmmm….

The Greatest Generation Makes People Feel Good

This is probably one of their greatest qualities.

Helping others realize their full potential, helping others who didn't have the advantages you may have had early in life, and giving a friend safe harbor in one of the many storms that life can bring are not only the right things to do but are immensely satisfying.

My dad did this for so many people.

The Men of the Greatest Generation Are Still Little Boys at Heart

There is no better example of this one than this famous saying: "The only difference between men and boys is the price of their toys."

Throughout his life, Dad and his friends knew how to have fun, and that quality stayed with him his entire life.

Much of today's generation has unfortunately taken this one too far. The car they drive, the home they live in, and the vacations they take seem to define them.

The greatest generation knew their responsibilities came first and then the toys.

The Greatest Generation Has So Many Real Friends

Their lives were filled with hard work and hard play.

They treated people with honesty and integrity and helped others every chance they got.

The result is a lifetime of people who consider themselves a friend.

There was standing room only at Dad’s funeral.

It made me proud.

The Greatest Generation Has Goals Most Feel Are Unreachable Or Unrealistic

But they built a nation with those unrealistically high goals... You can't imagine how many times I have been told my goals are unrealistic. Thanks, Dad.

The Greatest Generation Believes Imagination Is Stronger Than Knowledge

This one is very closely related to the previous page. The cliché that comes to mind is, "The person that says it can't be done is usually interrupted by someone doing it." They knew imagination meant everything.

It beats knowledge. It beats experience. Combined with a positive attitude and some serious commitment, it is responsible for every major accomplishment of man.

It allowed us to walk out of the cave, to explore the world, to take flight, to leave our planet, and set foot on another world. It has created technology that not very long ago would have been considered science fiction. It turns a business into an empire, an idea into a way of life. It gets you the beautiful woman; it turns sex into a fantasy. It's everything.

The Greatest Generation Believes in Hard Work

They believed in it, they weren't afraid of it, and, in fact, they embraced it!

It's a principle the younger generations seem to find so difficult to accept.

They believed in "paying their dues."

"There are no shortcuts."

"You have to put in the effort."

I thought that was so wrong when I was younger.

I was wrong.

The Greatest Generation Knows Real Power Is Never Given, Real Power Is Taken

This is another one of those sayings that offends the masses.

But as most complain about the blunt message and the political incorrectness of this philosophy, it is to those people who live it that everybody looks to in time of need.

The greatest generation knew how to acquire power, but they also knew how to keep it, or in many cases, keep it in the family.

And, Finally, the Greatest Generation Knows the Power of Having the Right Woman

Mom and Dad were married for fifty-three years before we lost Mom to cancer.

Was their marriage like Ward and June Cleaver's? No, it certainly was not. But they were there for each other.

They were high school sweethearts, and she was there when he returned from WWII.

She was there during good times and bad. When he made lots of money and when he didn't.

She put her children's and his needs before her own for her entire life.

And when we lost her, the loss he felt was excruciating.

She was a Greatest Generation Mom.

I can't imagine what my grandparents were going through when they read this:

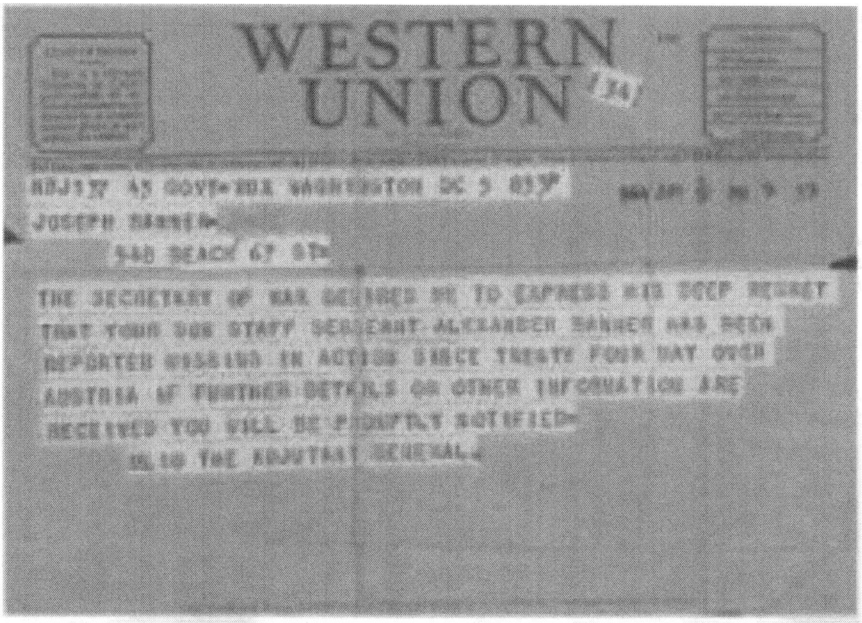

WESTERN UNION

[illegible] GOVT [illegible] WASHINGTON DC [illegible]

JOSEPH [illegible]

540 BEACH 67 ST

THE SECRETARY OF WAR DESIRES ME TO EXPRESS HIS DEEP REGRET THAT YOUR SON STAFF SERGEANT ALEXANDER [illegible] HAS BEEN REPORTED MISSING IN ACTION SINCE TWENTY FOUR MAY OVER AUSTRIA IF FURTHER DETAILS OR OTHER INFORMATION ARE RECEIVED YOU WILL BE PROMPTLY NOTIFIED=

[illegible] THE ADJUTANT GENERAL.

A certain amount of relief, for sure, but was he okay? Would they ever see him again?

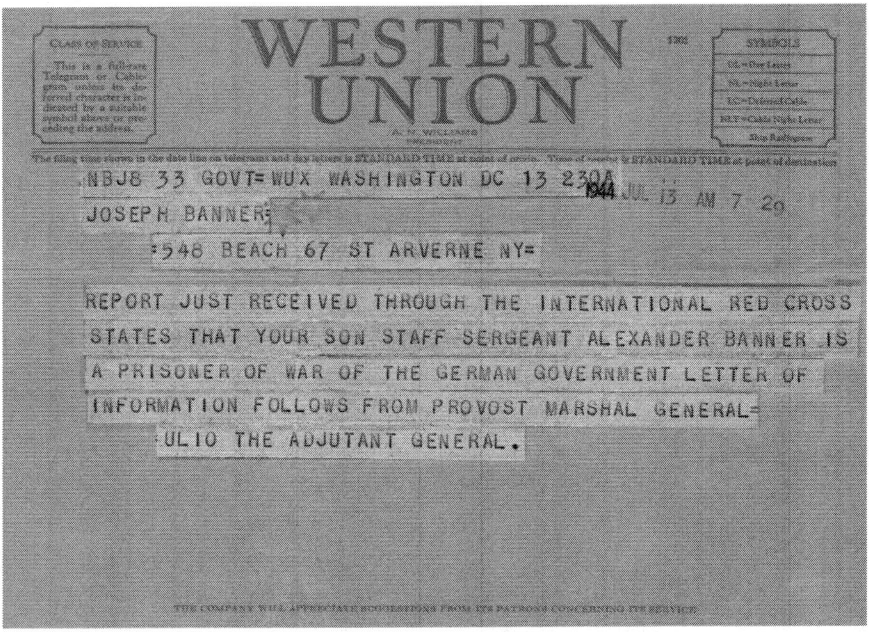

WESTERN UNION

NBJ8 33 GOVT=WUX WASHINGTON DC 13 230A
1944 JUL 13 AM 7 29

JOSEPH BANNER=

=548 BEACH 67 ST ARVERNE NY=

REPORT JUST RECEIVED THROUGH THE INTERNATIONAL RED CROSS STATES THAT YOUR SON STAFF SERGEANT ALEXANDER BANNER IS A PRISONER OF WAR OF THE GERMAN GOVERNMENT LETTER OF INFORMATION FOLLOWS FROM PROVOST MARSHAL GENERAL=

ULIO THE ADJUTANT GENERAL.

Back in American control! I was more than a decade away from being born, but I can see the tears in both my grandparent's eyes when they read that.

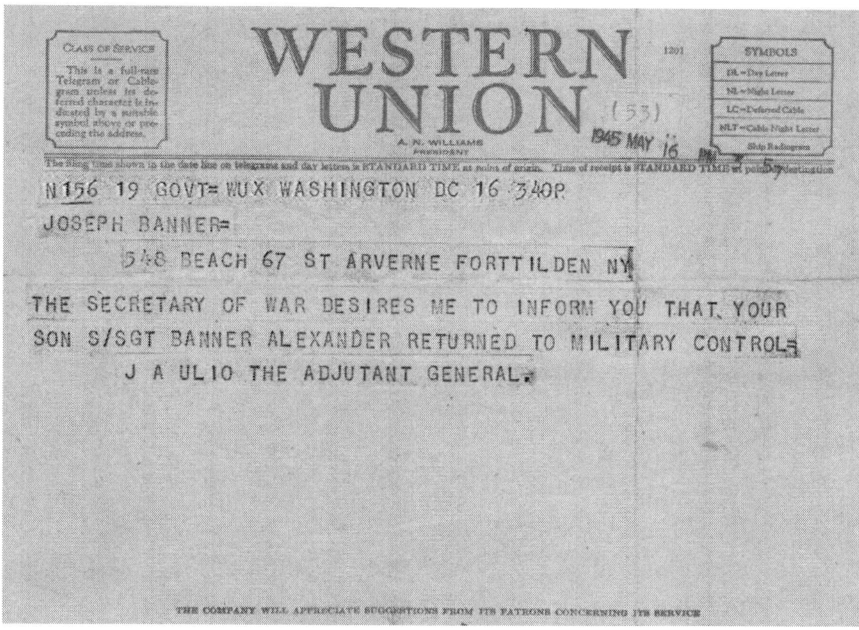

CLASS OF SERVICE
This is a full-rate Telegram or Cablegram unless its deferred character is indicated by a suitable symbol above or preceding the address.

WESTERN UNION

A. N. WILLIAMS PRESIDENT

1201

SYMBOLS
DL = Day Letter
NL = Night Letter
LC = Deferred Cable
NLT = Cable Night Letter
Ship Radiogram

(53)

1945 MAY 16 PM

N156 19 GOVT=WUX WASHINGTON DC 16 340P

JOSEPH BANNER=

548 BEACH 67 ST ARVERNE FORTTILDEN NY

THE SECRETARY OF WAR DESIRES ME TO INFORM YOU THAT YOUR SON S/SGT BANNER ALEXANDER RETURNED TO MILITARY CONTROL=

J A ULIO THE ADJUTANT GENERAL.

THE COMPANY WILL APPRECIATE SUGGESTIONS FROM ITS PATRONS CONCERNING ITS SERVICE

“Be home tomorrow night.” How many sons sent that message? How many didn’t?

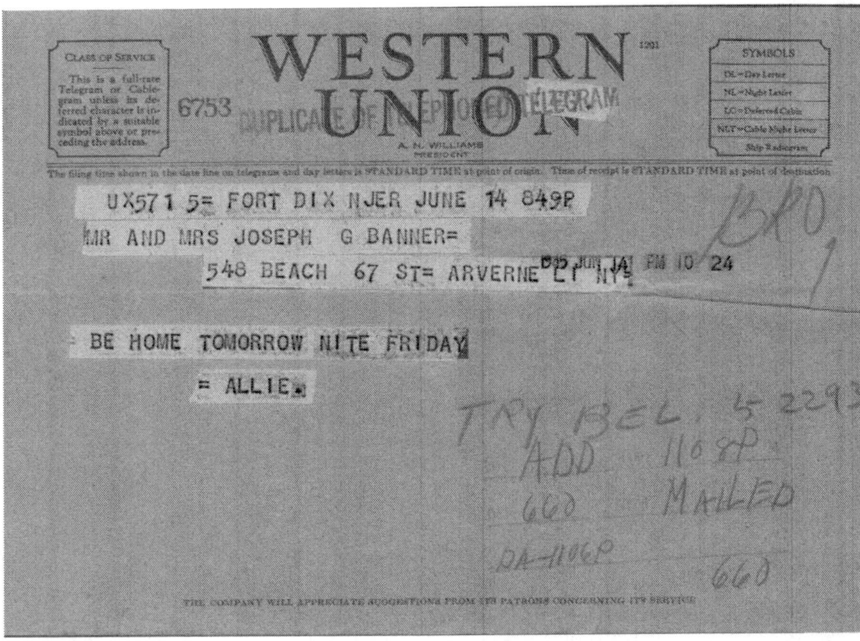

WESTERN UNION

CLASS OF SERVICE
This is a full-rate Telegram or Cablegram unless its deferred character is indicated by a suitable symbol above or preceding the address.

6753 DUPLICATE OF TELEPHONED TELEGRAM

A. N. WILLIAMS
PRESIDENT

SYMBOLS
DL=Day Letter
NL=Night Letter
LC=Deferred Cable
NLT=Cable Night Letter
Ship Radiogram

The filing time shown in the date line on telegrams and day letters is STANDARD TIME at point of origin. Time of receipt is STANDARD TIME at point of destination

UX571 5= FORT DIX NJER JUNE 14 849P
MR AND MRS JOSEPH G BANNER=
548 BEACH 67 ST= ARVERNE LI NY=

BE HOME TOMORROW NITE FRIDAY
= ALLIE.

THE COMPANY WILL APPRECIATE SUGGESTIONS FROM ITS PATRONS CONCERNING ITS SERVICE

An article in a New York newspaper mentions my Dad and his older brother, Phil, another greatest generation hero, recuperating in a hospital in the South Pacific.

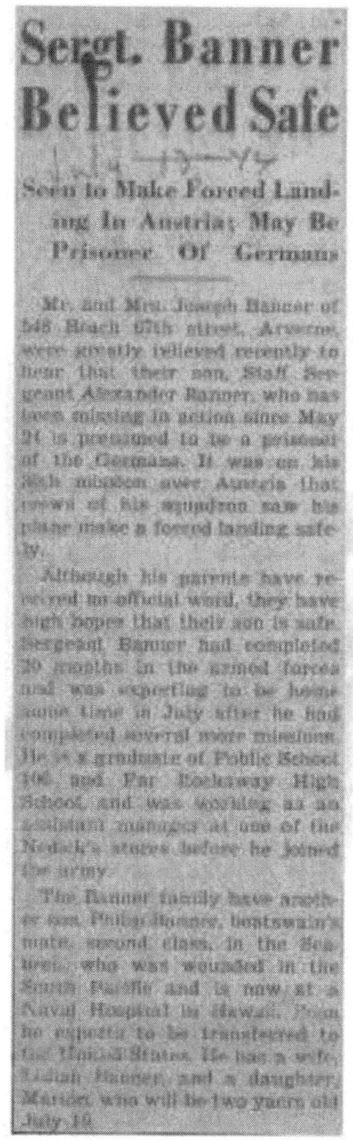

Sergt. Banner Believed Safe

Seen to Make Forced Landing In Austria; May Be Prisoner Of Germans

Mr. and Mrs. Joseph Banner of 548 Beach 67th street, Arverne, were greatly relieved recently to hear that their son, Staff Sergeant Alexander Banner, who has been missing in action since May 24 is presumed to be a prisoner of the Germans. It was on his [illegible] mission over Austria that crews of his squadron saw his plane make a forced landing safely.

Although his parents have received no official word, they have high hopes that their son is safe. Sergeant Banner had completed 20 months in the armed forces and was expecting to be home some time in July after he had completed several more missions. He is a graduate of Public School 106 and Far Rockaway High School, and was working as an assistant manager at one of the Nedick's stores before he joined the army.

The Banner family have another son, Philip Banner, boatswain's mate, second class, in the Seabees, who was wounded in the South Pacific and is now at a Naval Hospital in Hawaii. From [illegible] he expects to be transferred to the United States. He has a wife, Lillian Banner, and a daughter, Marion, who will be two years old July 19.

A Certificate of Appreciation given to my Dad and all that returned home victorious.

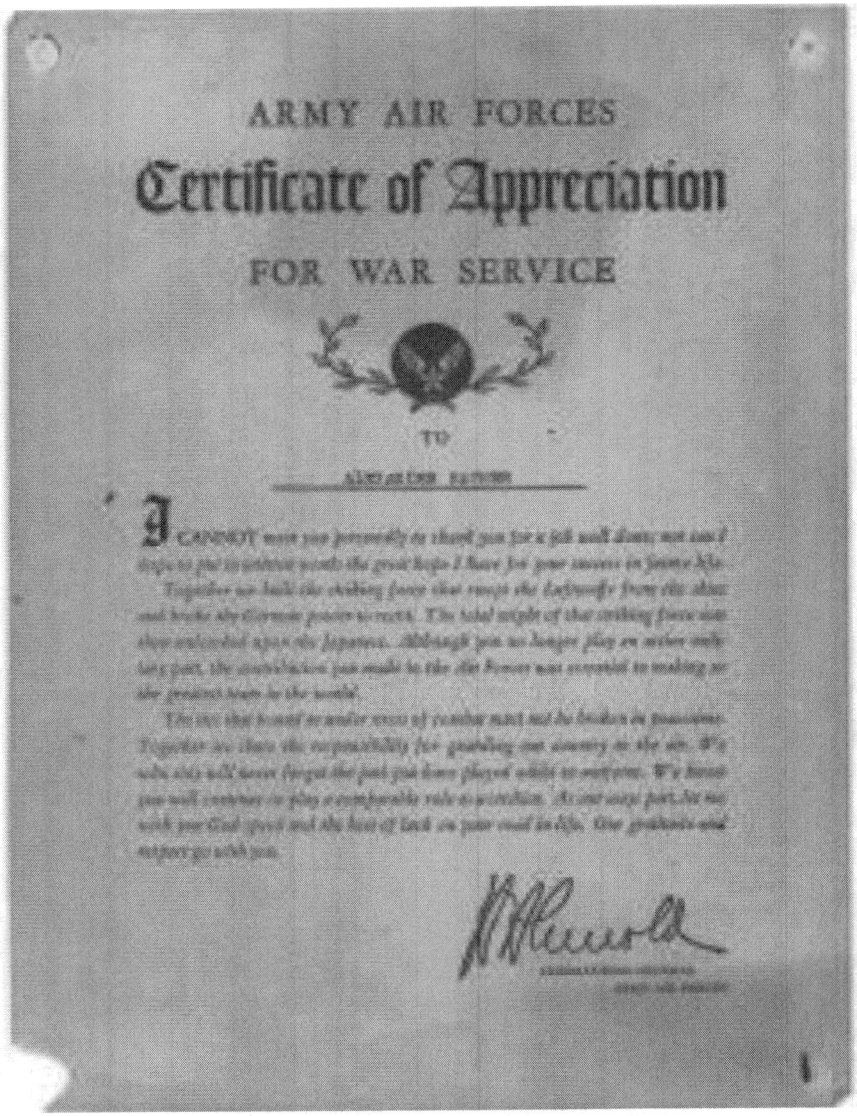

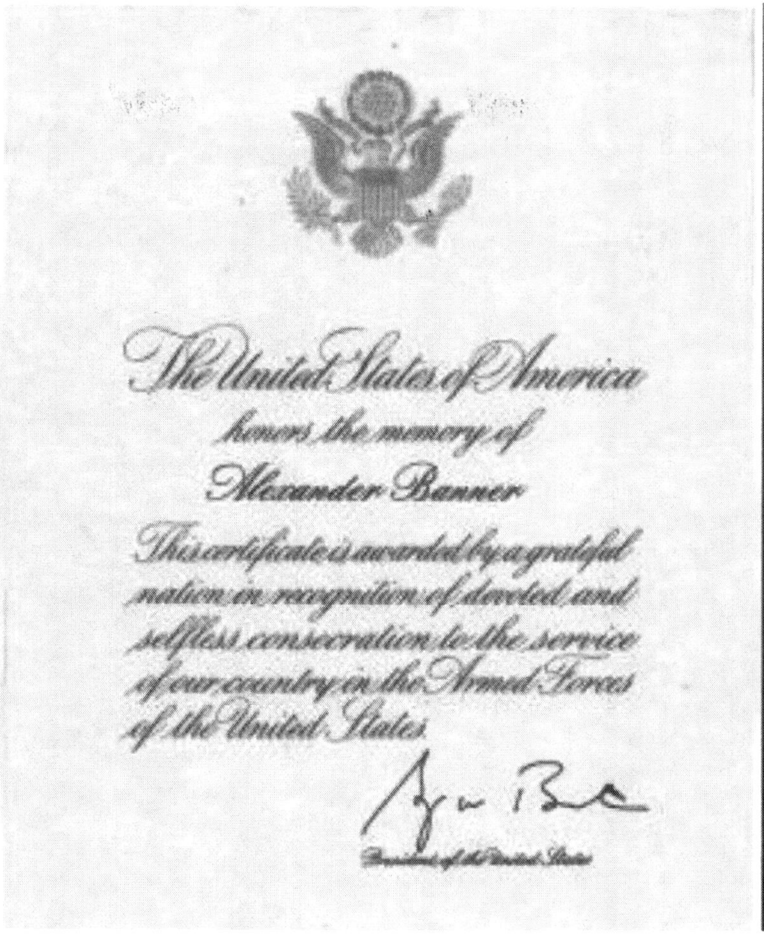

The United States of America

honors the memory of

Alexander Banner

This certificate is awarded by a grateful nation in recognition of devoted and selfless consecration to the service of our country in the Armed Forces of the United States.

President of the United States

Like so many others, he went to war as a boy but came back as a man.

So proud of his country, he returned to the girl he left behind. They were married for 53 years.

Dad and I out for dinner. That smile was always on his face.

Mom and Dad right before my wedding ☺ Okay, fine, one of my weddings...

This picture was taken at Dad's 70th birthday party. On his right is his youngest brother, Norm, and on his left is his brother, Sid.

Look at the smiles on their faces. Those smiles came from knowing they had all served their country proudly, built successful businesses, and, more importantly, been incredible role models for their children. Even though they are all gone now, I feel their presence every day.

A 21-gun salute and a lone trumpet playing taps for a hero.

Today's best of the best showing their honor and respect for their predecessors. I could see Dad smiling...

About The Author

Originally from New York, Mike has lived in Florida for most of his life.

A single dad to his 3 children, most of his life, which he feels is his greatest achievement. And now being "Poppy" to his 4 grandchildren takes the highest priority.

A well-known national and accomplished speaker in his 40+ year mortgage career, host of the 62 Who Knew Television Show, and now published author, Mike has appeared on National television, radio and in numerous publications as an expert on the topic of increasing the quality of life for seniors.

He attributes his perspective in life to his father, who taught him the ways of the Greatest Generation.

Made in the USA
Columbia, SC
26 May 2025

58460626R00035